Elsewhere, we Became

By
Ari Augustine

Cover Design by
Katherine Manolios

Also by Ari Augustine

A SPARK IN THE NIGHT

ISBN: 0692097821
ISBN-13: 978-0692097823

DEDICATION

***

For my friends who,
above all else,
gave me a home.

And for Harry,
who saw hope
among the ruins.

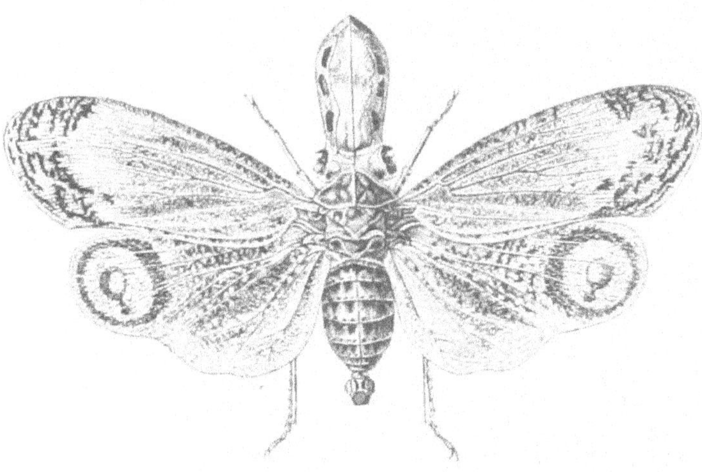

CONTENTS

The Little e	10
Accountability	12
Untitled	13
Torn Petals	14
Ornery	16
Summer days	19
You	20
The wound between child and adult	22
Keep this piece for you	24
Morse Code Confessions	25
Beautiful words	26
How to break a heart	27
A ghost	28
Don't settle	29
Forgiveness	30
Safe	32
Irreconcilable Differences	34
The end	36
Is a beginning	37
The cost of happiness	38
Chipped & Chiseled	39
Querencia	40
F-BOMB	42

Pride	44
What I needed you to say	46
Gasoline	47
Sonder	48
Beauty & the beast	50
Carousel Island	52
The right question	54
Firefly	56
What is beauty?	58
picasso: blue period	60
not enough	61
Broken hearts	62
PTSD	64
Perspective	65
Cathedral	66
The definition of love	69
Vulnerable	70
Limitations	72
Wandering hearts	73
Lovers	74
Hornet's nest	76
Becoming	77
I am not a vessel	78
Under siege	80
Hope	83

The Anatomy of Memory	84
Graffitti	86
Fruhling des Bedauern	87
City soup	88
Fences	89
Loaded heart	91
Persistence	93
Needs	94
You can't erase it	97
Eleutheromania	98
Keep it to yourself	100
Just say no	101
Amaranthine	103
Finder's fee	104
Chromatic Aberration	106
Alleyway	107
Logophile	108
Depression	109
Smile	110
Ruined	111
The Perfectionist	112
ORIGAMI	113
Los Angeles	114
If it's worth it	116
V	116

Desire 118

Hurricane 119

21st street 120

Anxious Soul 121

Muse 122

How we end 123

All I know is this 124

Reckless Abandon 125

Undone 127

Things I should tell you 128

Loose Connection 129

Kintsugi 130

ENCORE: 131

Overcome 132

Shades of blue 133

I love the way I hate you 134

Welcomed lies 135

ACKNOWLEDGEMENTS 137

ABOUT THE AUTHOR 138

ABOUT THE COVER-DESIGNER 139

ABOUT THE ILLUSTRATIONS 140

The Little e

***

Untitled was the first poem I'd written. Its lines crooked and without symmetry,
words pressed tight against the page,
unable to breathe.

You could follow the dark shadows of graphite and lead, trace the awkward, childish pause where I left a comma instead of a period.

Where I abandoned the line, everything open,
the vulnerable arm of a little "e" reaching out over the emptiness of the page below.

It was a poem I'd written for my mother.

It was a poem I composed countless times, but water ruined the words. Water and hopes and questions that wouldn't stop. I tore each version and they burned, ashes to ashes.
Dust to dust.

My counselor said it would be cathartic, the act of handwriting unyielding
thoughts in my mind might help me to
forgive or forget.

I watched the little "e" glow like the cherry of a cigarette, bright at first.
It didn't last and as soon as it burst into life, thick puffs of white smoke invaded.

The scent of burning paper was acrid, welcome.

It soaked into the fabric of my clothes, my hair, my skin. It reminded me of Holiday Acres
and a sea of trees; of tobacco, bobby pins, and pine sap that glued itself to bare knuckles.

I was enveloped in an overwhelming desire to reminiscence, to speak of all the things I missed: the loose floor boards that always creaked at night,

even with no one else around.

The sharp, uneven teeth of a brush that worked knots from my hair. Though the ritual hurt, my skull ached for it. I longed for the scent of biscuits & gravy and listened in the morning for the loud shout, the wake-up warning.

It never came and my ears yearned for it.

I never said anything as the poem steadily blackened leaving behind the pillow-soft ashes.
They resembled cremated remains and I felt this was poetic. Death, after all, possessed many forms. I gathered the ashes, not caring if they painted me in a thin layer of gray dust or stained my knees. I wanted to touch them, to feel their presence,

to know why or how or who.

I imagined the little "e" was in there somewhere, lost, not destroyed. I felt the charcoal ash cake beneath my fingernails. I felt it in my throat, my lungs, my eyes.

Water ruined everything.
It left streaks of ash and memory across my face, imbrued the flesh of my body with words I couldn't express, capture, decode.

I'd written an imperfect poem, lines as crooked as my memory, edges as abrupt as a child self, and like my heart,
it was without symmetry.

Accountability

***

Why do
we always
blame the outsider,
the other man
or
other woman,
instead of the one
who let them in?

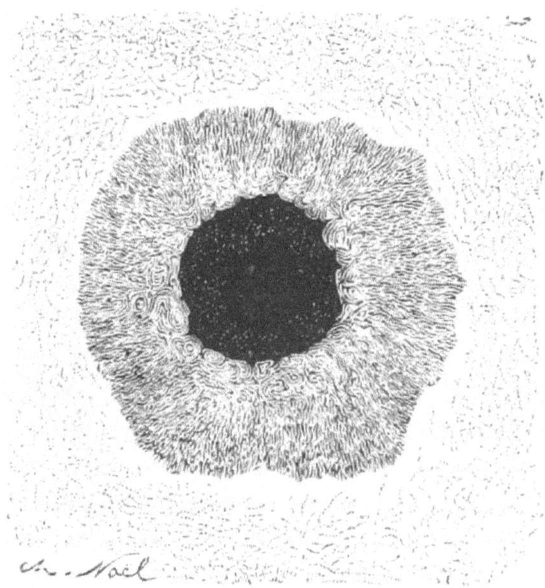

(16 juin.) Tache solaire observ

Untitled

***

No longer do I waste precious time
Trying to be the opposite of who I am.
If you cannot love me,
The fault isn't mine.

ich make such a brave show yonder, are replaced here

AINU WOMAN OF FRISHIKOBETS, ON THE TOKACHI RIVER.

Torn Petals

***

I try to imagine the feeling she must have felt, back pressed into a plastic chair and listening to the mutterings of a doctor.

> "You suffer from episodes."
> "You have fits of rage."
> "You're uncontrollable."
> "You need help. We can help you."

And he writes her life in his little black book: *10 year old girl. Chubby. Despondent. Blunt affect. Does not understand weight of her actions. Increase doses.* And he tells her this is no life for a child, that her entire family suffers because of her refusal to change at the snap of a finger.

I try to imagine her alone in a room, terrified to look in the mirror and see a fractured reflection -- jagged, uneven, unworthy of salvaging. The spine of her life's little book already worn and broken, clinging to unwritten pages. I imagine she would tear them out, fold them into origami sculptures. She would suffer the papercuts to express what words couldn't capture:

White flower. Clumsily torn petals. Fingerprints, like blood red bruises.

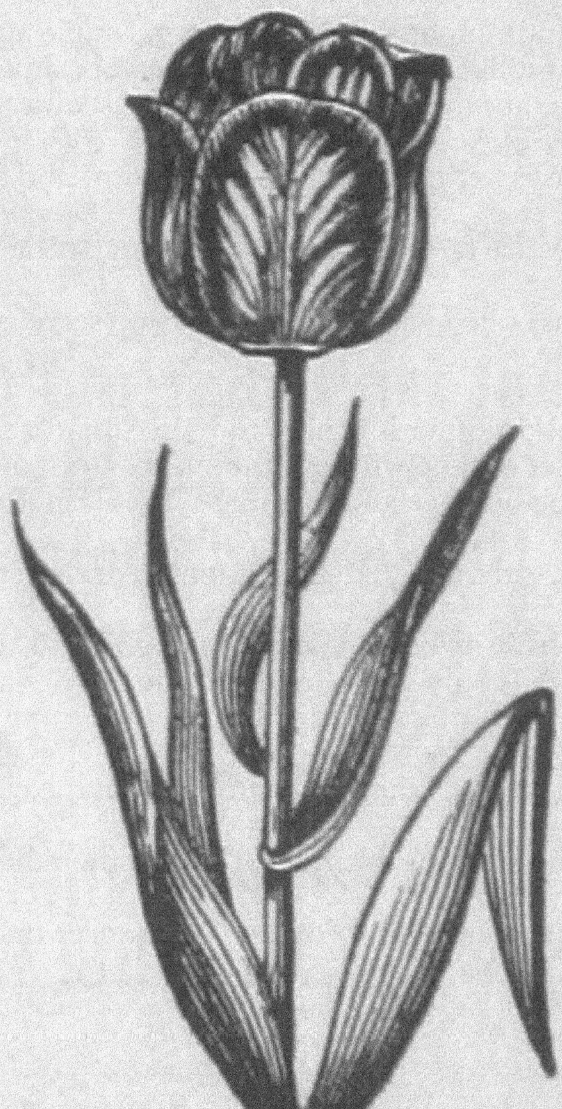

Ornery

***

My Grandmother says I am ornery. I smile at the word.
She says it like a compliment as she, too, smiles.
And she taps the end of cigarette to cast away the ashes.

She chases her thoughts out the window and across the yard.
Her eyes are far away and the lines on her face a lovely map,
A canvass filled with secrets but it's no secret she has cancer.

My Grandmother is ornery too. We smile at the word.
She gazes out the window, the smoke from the cigarette
Clouding her face and forming symbols in the air.

I try to read them, like divination, to decipher the map of her life.
Where had she been? Where is she going? Is there time?
But there is only smoke and fire and the defiance lit in her eyes.

"You're ornery," she says, stamping out the cigarette and swatting
Away the remains of smoke. I realize then that she is talking to herself.
My Grandmother is too ornery for cancer to beat her.

"He arose and rebuked the Winds and the Sea"

Summer days

***

In the beginning, she wanted to escape.

She wanted to take her little sister's hand and disappear into the mouth of the forest, sunlight at her back like a cape of courage. She wanted the mud pies they made to feed the hungriest holes in hearts and for the night time to bathe them in a starlight concoction of dreams that would make them forget.

She wanted to sit beside that fire forever, stories tasting like wood smoke and burnt marshmallows on her tongue. Together, they inhaled the warm air, unafraid of the darkness because she guarded them with a wooden sword and heart of steel. Because the fire embedded her lungs with embers and together, they could breathe fire.

In the beginning, she wanted summer to last forever. She wished for it on four leaf clovers. She drew them into the rusty orange dirt and built shrines to faeries, luring them with sweet promises and pieces of candy. She wished on shooting stars and pressed her hands in prayer and bargained with her life.

And the day her wooden sword shattered to splinters in the garden beneath the oldest pine tree of the forest and the sun no longer gave her the cloak of courage, they knew that summer was over.

As they packed their bags and stood in the garden, they saw the leaves had turned from green to red, leaving trees stripped and naked as earthy veins reaching for the sky. And she smiled at its rugged beauty, the way it was caught in a twisted, knotted pose of refusal to yield completely to the elements. "I know how you feel," she whispered, and then, they were gone.

You

***

Don't listen to them when they speak for your pain.
They'll do their best to convince you that the past has
nothing to do with who you are; it has everything to
do with the person you've become,
with the scars you bear,
the places you go,
the life you envision,
all the little imperfections,
and I love you all the
more for it.

STAR WITH AURORA.

The wound between child and adult

***

As a child, you told me I
Was capable of anything.
Adventures.
Dreams.
Love.
All of it was in the palm
Of my tiny, trembling hand.
As an adult, you tell me I
Would have to be 1 in 1,000,000.
I am capable of anything -
Adventure.
Dreams.
Love.
Only if I'm lucky.

I wonder who convinced you
Of your own incapability
To be amazing
At whatever
Makes your
Heart
Sing.

Keep this piece for you

***

risk it

lose, start again

never

force your heart

To serve

Morse Code Confessions

***

.. / .- -- / .- ..-. .-. .- .. -.. / -- -.-- / .-.. .. ..-. . / .-- .. .-.. .-.. / -- . .- -. / -.
--- - .... .. -. --. .-.-.- / .. / .-- .- -. - / -.-- --- ..- / - --- / .-. . -- . -- -... . .-.
/ .. / .-- .- ... / .... . .-. . .-.-.-

I am afraid my life will mean nothing. I want you to remember I was here.

Beautiful words

***

I love you.

I never understood the words until they clung to your lips like a kiss.

How to break a heart

***

Make promises you have no intention to keep.

A ghost

***

My little sister, Lena, was sound asleep. I could hear her breathing softly, her nose making tiny whistles as she rolled to her side, gathering her arms and legs into her chest. Her hands were curled into fists as she gripped the blankets possessively. Her long, dark chestnut hair tangled around her face but it didn't matter. Even in the dark, I knew she was smiling.

I kissed her forehead, hoping she was dreaming of a different world; a kinder world. With my suitcase in tow, stuffed with decisions I have made, I left just as I arrived: a ghost.

Don't settle

***

People keep asking me how I am happy and passionate. I tell them it's simple: do what you love.

Do it for you and don't apologize or settle for anything less than what is genuinely adored by your heart.

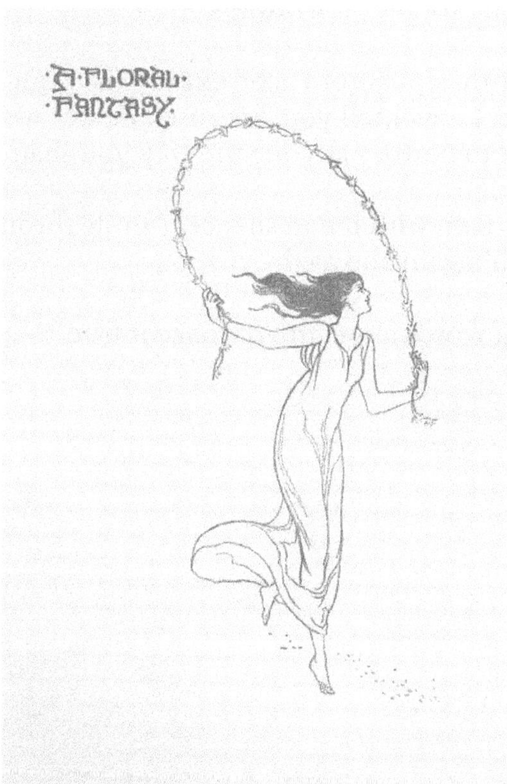

Forgiveness

***

I wish letting go and moving on was easier; that I could understand the reasons you abandoned me to the wilds of the world, but there's a splinter in my heart that aches when I try to remove it.

"Don't forget", it whispers.

I feel it spasm, a phantom ache exactly the same as the day you put it there. I never tell you, because I do not want to hurt you. I never want to destroy anyone the way you shattered me.

I carry this pain with me in silence, I smile through it, I say "I forgive you" again and again.

As if words alone might make it true.

Amaryllis formosissima.

Safe

***

Our bed is where I am safe.
In the cornflower yellow of sunlight
bleeding in, enveloped by your scent
clinging to my pillow,
we fit together - a jigsaw of
arms, legs, the napes of necks -
anchored to peaceful shores.

Irreconcilable Differences

***

There was a time
When I would have folded my body
Parallel to yours, become a mirror of
Your desires, however black.
Against my nature, I would have chewed
Words, sealed my eyes shut, turned the
Other cheek because I loved you.
In the worst ways, I needed the creases,
The worn lines you left on me from the
Folding, all the bending it took to fit
The form you desired in me.
And it was only when I became tough,
Unmalleable, inflexible from overworking,
That I found the courage to open my
Eyes, to crawl out of the mirror, and
Unfold myself, limb by limb, from
Your embrace.
You are nothing but hectic creases and
Folds in the fabric of my life that I,
For all the pain you've caused, couldn't quite
Iron out completely.

The end

***

The worst part was never knowing why we stopped being friends. It was wondering if, after all, I was too damaged or strange to hold you in my life. I gave you pieces of myself, a bouquet of imperfections, and you threw me away.

I believed I was the moth who needed the warmth of your flame. With all of my heart, I despaired at the idea that I snuffed you out because all that remained between us was smoke.

Is a beginning

***

The best part was coming up for air; it was hearing the call of contagious laughter, feeling an embrace of security and acceptance as I discovered there was life after you. With new friends, I built new pieces of myself, fashioned them out every moment I could hold. I'd been recycled, reborn, restored.

And it was them who taught me that I was not the moth drawn to the brightest flames. I was not a ghost, a spectre clinging to places I did not belong. With all my heart, I wept in happiness. I sighed with relief because the smoke had finally cleared and
I was not alone.

The cost of happiness

***

~~falling in love with her. Petra Cotes,~~
~~for her part, loved him more and~~
~~more as~~ she felt his love ~~increasing,~~
~~and that was how in~~ the ripeness ~~of~~
~~autumn she began to believe once~~
~~more in the~~ youthful superstition
that ~~poverty was the servitude of~~
~~love. Both looked back then on the~~
wild revelry, ~~the gaudy wealth~~,
and ~~the unbridled fornication as~~
~~an annoyance and they lamented~~
~~that~~ it ~~had~~ cost them ~~so much of~~
~~their lives to find the~~ paradise ~~of~~
~~shared~~ solitude. ~~Madly in love after~~
~~so many years of sterile complicity,~~
~~they enjoyed the miracle of living~~
~~each other as much at the table~~
~~as in bed, and they grew~~ to be so
happy ~~that even when they were~~
~~two worn out people they kept on~~
~~blooming like little children and~~
~~playing together like dogs.~~

Chipped & Chiseled

***

~~If~~ you ~~can~~ keep ~~your head when all~~
~~about you~~
~~Are~~ losing ~~theirs and blaming it on~~
~~you,~~
~~If you can trust~~ yourself ~~when all~~
~~men doubt you,~~
~~But make allowance for their~~
~~doubting too;~~
~~If you can wait and not be tired by~~
~~waiting,~~
~~Or being lied about, dont deal in~~
~~lies,~~
~~Or being hated, dont give way~~ to
~~hating,~~
~~And yet dont~~ look ~~too~~ good, ~~nor talk~~

Querencia

***

The life I have is not the life I wanted; It is the life I have always needed.

I'm so incredibly lucky to have a wonderful husband, to have the ability to travel the world, the means to educate myself, little indulgences to remind me that life can be kind, and the horizon, which was once seemingly out of my reach, so close that I can feel the sun's warmth before it bows to the moon.

This is not the life I wanted but it is the life I love and need. And all the people in it, those that I adore, and all the adventures taking place, these are what make me happy.

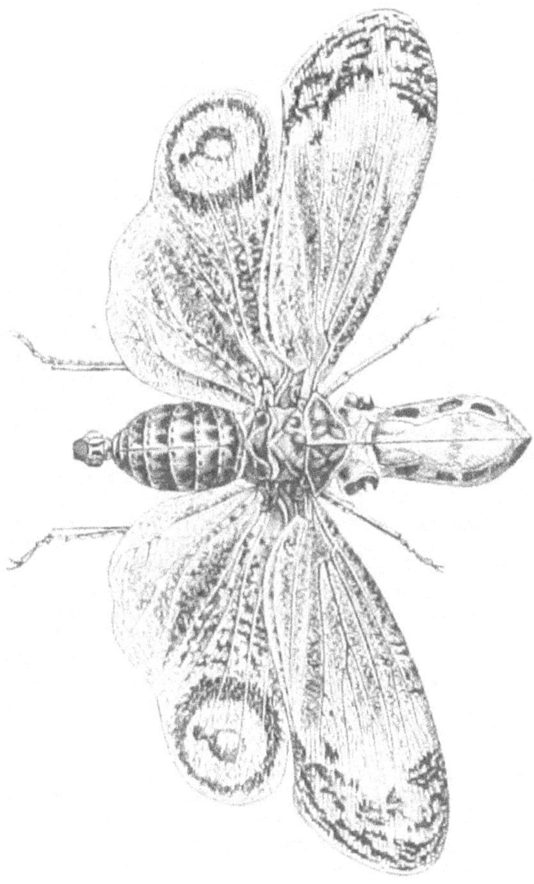

F-BOMB

***

I am a woman
and I own my life
my body
my thoughts
my desires.
I am a daughter.
of a daughter
of a daughter,
who were less fortunate than I.

Those daughters weren't allowed to
read
vote
study math or science
chose their partners
defend themselves
own their bodies
say **NO**

I am a sister
to three other women
who are more fortunate than our ancestors
but are still told
what to do with their bodies
who to love
how to look attractive
to settle for less than men
they are not 'built' for labor
& aren't 'wired' for math or science
It's 2018.

I am a woman
I am a daughter
I am a sister
I am a feminist

Pride

***

There is a way back home from here
I forgot the path long ago, I fear.

I'd wait for silver-threaded signs.
I'd walk in circles for eternal miles.
I would call out into darkened lines
Of trees that stalked me in the night.

I'd scorn the sun jeering from the sky,
I'd blame the dust lodged in my eye.
Add someone gave me bad advice.
I'd wonder why, I'd wonder why.

But in all my fear and half-hearted acts,
I'd likely choose not to double back,
Revisit the once familiar path and see,
If there's something I missed
In my hurry to leave.

CHÂTEAU DE B

tel qu'il devait être en 1430, d'après

What I needed you to say

***

Our love was bitter and cruel, as if infected by a poison on the arrow cupid drove into our hearts. Our love was a season, a breeze, a half-hearted promise never intended to be kept.

We stole precious time with kisses, each sweeping our tongues to cleanse the acrid lies we told, the aftertaste of our acetous mistakes lingering on our lips.

We fought. We cheated. We lied. We stole. We broke each other down like legos in the park, an audience of friends and family who could not reach us with reason.

As long as someone held on, no one was free.

You asked me what could have been said that would have spared us, what path could we have taken to reclaim the best we'd stolen from each other. And I claimed there was nothing to be done.
Love was love, no matter how monstrous,
bitter,
cruel,
unkind.

Years later, I finally have the words you needed to utter:

Say you never loved me. Say I meant nothing and leave. Never call again, even when we're so lonely it aches, no matter how many messages I leave on your voicemail. Do not smile or laugh or pretend we can be friends because we're not; we're enemies.

Let's become ghosts to each other, make believe friends who pass each other like ships in the night, averting our eyes as we disappear into the fog of life and forget either one of us existed.

Whatever you choose to say, do it quickly and surely, and when you leave, don't look back to see me crumble. Because what I need more than your words is closure and if I see through the lies, I won't learn to let go.

Gasoline

***

I don't know why I remember the smell of gasoline. Sitting on the garage floor in nothing but my short corduroys, grease smeared on my knees, I watch Papa curse over the truck engine. Gasoline, sawdust, and grease was all over the garage, painting it with the leftovers of hard work and, often, failed attempts.

Carved wooden projects were stacked against the shells of cars, which were bursting with old, odd bits from the house. Shelves in the corner held an assortment of paint and were lined with Folgers Coffee cans overflowing with nuts, bolts, and nails.

I sat, leaning against the metal shell of a station wagon, entertaining myself with toy cars. These were distractions I most likely stole from my uncle when he wasn't in his room. A wrench slams into the engine and I drop my toys.

Papa, in the stream of curses, storms out of the garage, tearing the door off its hinges. I stand there, as light invades the dim space, bringing with it a fresh breath - a breeze.

But all I can smell is gasoline.

Sonder

***

She failed to notice your small
hands at the nape of her neck.
Your breath was unsteady as you
proclaimed your affections.
A fool in love with an oblivious
Wonder.

Your words were drops of rain
pelting a bright red umbrella.
Where your eyes held hope,
she saw friendliness.
An oblivious wonder captured
in the gaze of a fool in love.

Beauty & the beast

***

I cannot pretend

you didn't break my heart,
you didn't teach me how cruel
a love could be.

I cannot deny

the anger I held toward you
the pity and empathy
the emotions you drew from me
like water from a well.

I cannot forgive

and forget,
live and let go,
abandon hope.

I cannot lie
and say I do not love
the monster in you.

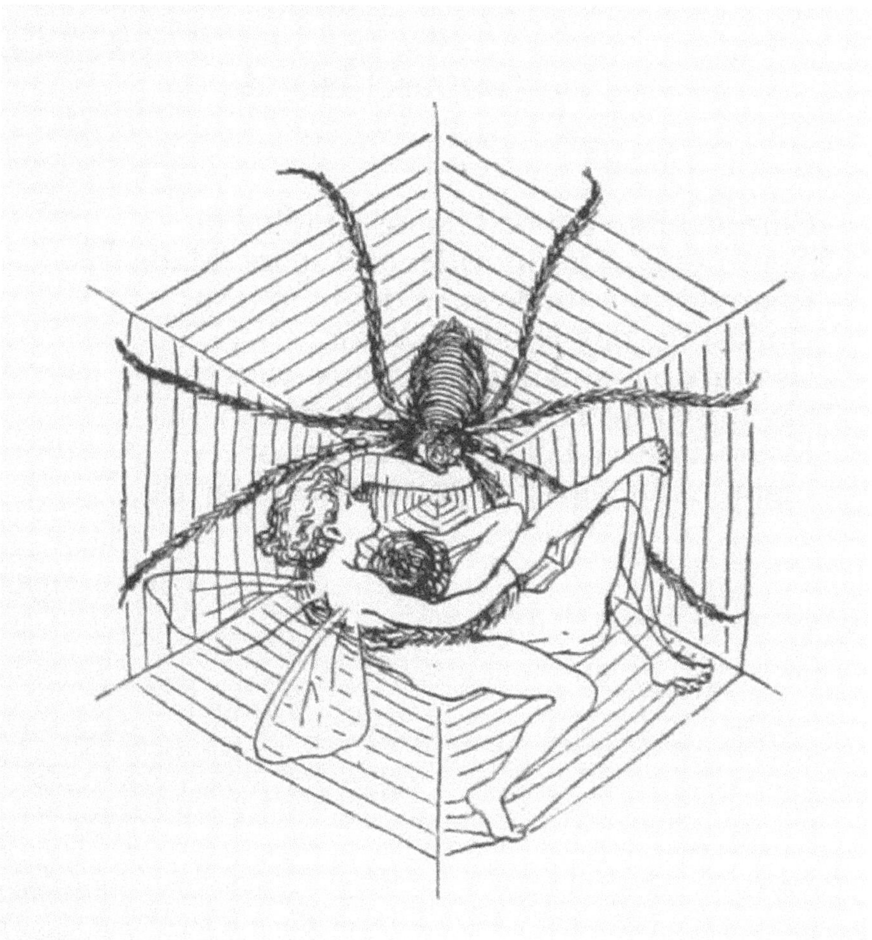

Carousel Island

***

Climbed into cupped hands, cradled in
Arguments of gunpowder and spark. Made
Room for the shadows of doubt in heart.
Outlast the day. Find a way for
Us to fix our sinking ship, water-wrecked.
Say it isn't over. Say we're better than this.
Every time we fail to see a flicker of
Light in our capsized union, sink or swim.

THE OPEN SEA.

The right question

***

"What do you need?" I stared at him. The question came as puzzle pieces, fitting to answers blooming inside me.

To be loved, I replied in my head. *To be needed and known. To be heard and held and wanted. To feel beyond anger and sadness. To look in the mirror and see someone I can be proud of, not the daughter of a daughter of a daughter, who did all the wrong things.*

tain. And now, among the spectators there commenced

MOON APPROACHING THE SUN.

Firefly

***

I remember you saying you wished you knew me,
and that I could see the kindness you saw when you
looked at me.

It was the day it wouldn't stop raining and we
chased each other around in the yard, abandoning
the heaviness of our clothing.

You kissed me but
all I could taste was the summer rain infused
with tobacco.

bittersweet, you said.
A beginning and an end.

You came to find me that night and said you loved
me and it clung in the air, lingering in your breath.

a firefly, you said.
A single word trapped in your head.

He finds her, and this is the consequence.

What is beauty?

***

I wish I knew why we were unkind to ourselves. Why each triumph was weighed down by little slights that made it impossible to be good enough. After a while, no one had to say,

> "You should be thinner."
> "You should be smarter."
> "You should be prettier."

We took the razor words and did it to ourselves, all in the name of being better than whatever we were - in becoming plastic wonder women propped on a shelf and admired. In hindsight, we didn't even know what "beauty" was -- just that it wasn't us.

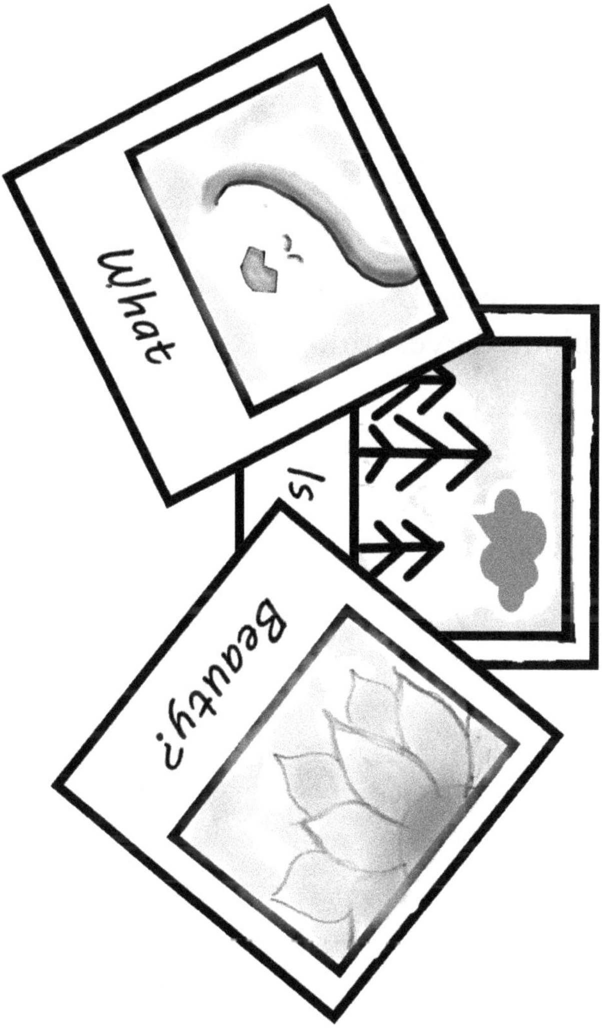
What
Is
Beauty?

picasso: blue period

***

Last night, I heard a reflection say,
"Who are you, anyways?"
I leaned over a puddle and saw it
frowning at me from the sky.
I couldn't fathom why streetlights
Brightened a face I saw dissolved in
Tears.
"Picasso," I answered,
As if it explained everything.

not enough

***

Life has taught me words are not enough.
Oxygen and gravity are not enough.
Religion and beliefs are not enough.
Desire and needs are not enough.
Truth and facts are not enough.
Love, alone, is not enough.
You and I are not enough.

Broken hearts

***

When I was small, I longed to know why.
Why wasn't I wanted.
Why wasn't I good enough.
Why wasn't I kept.
Why wasn't I loved.
When I was small, I thought of little else
except grief, emptiness, hunger.
Now, I am older, and I visit that small child.
I see the fissures in her heart,
I hear cries in my ears.
I feel her starving hands clutch me, fish hooks.
And I want to say why, to fill her with words
to muffle the sounds of life.
but I know now that all the reasons in the world
would not unbreak this heart.

PTSD

***

Her body will break like jar,
Spilling the contents of
Pickled words, candied-ginger
Filling the base of a saucer like
Rocks cast into a Seer's pond.

Her words are vessels,
Cargo ships bursting with
Memorabilia photographs,
Motives tacked to cork boards
Falling apart, she opens her
Mouth, nothing right comes out.

Her eyes are the soul,
Cerulean blue lines on a map,
Compasses with eager needles,
Never pointing South of
Her thinned lips clamping
Against combustion, fractured irises
Cutting words into confetti before
They've the chance to escape.

Perspective

***

As I move forward in life and look back, the world, which once felt incredibly large and consuming, is now small and almost unseen. It is as if the universe had tucked it, like a leaf, between the pages of a rather large book and the only time I ever really see it is if I happen across it without meaning to.

Cathedral

***

There is no common ground between us but I'm an architect. I would build a bridge to you. I would carve a deep path from the tips of my fingers to yours.

I would risk splinters and pitfalls to build our cathedral, a cradle for us to rest our weary heads, a sacred string of words as we breathe into each other.

You would be the first and final nail in the coffin, a reason to stay right where I am. I'd take the light you pour into me and use it to illuminate the space. I want you to see every inch of me.

There is no common ground between my body and yours but you're an artist. You would draw the quickest route to my heart with your lips. You would map the second we knew.

I would risk getting lost on a crooked back road. I would find the courage to say it this time. The dust of our trail would spin with maps of where we've been and a promise,

We'll keep going until there is nowhere else to run but into each other, closing the distance, the empty space that divides.
I would risk it all to hear your heart sing with mine.

The definition of love

***

I remember every day you uttered that sentence:
"This isn't love."
I thought you meant that I didn't understand love,
Or we weren't really in love, our desires doomed from page one.
I was unable hear what you couldn't say:
"This isn't the love you deserve."

Vulnerable

***

How does it make you feel? I desired to reply, more than anything, with reassurance. "I'm fine," were the words lingering, bitter lies clinging to my lips as my head spun with the innumerable triggers set off. I never could figure out why it was near impossible to admit my life was a sinking ship. I was constantly on edge, watching and waiting for inevitable danger.

My heart, the compass of my existence - and survival - spun without reason. Did she mean to ask, "How does it feel to think about the past?" Or perhaps she meant, "How does it feel to confront the possibility of failure?" Her question grew like a weed in my body, invasive, stamping out the light with the weight of "what ifs" and "could have beens". The sudden vastness of her words startled me. *How does it make you feel?*

Terrified. Out of control. A flower petal abandoned in a monsoon, delicate in the hands of a world gone mad.

ie landeseigentümliche Vegeta-

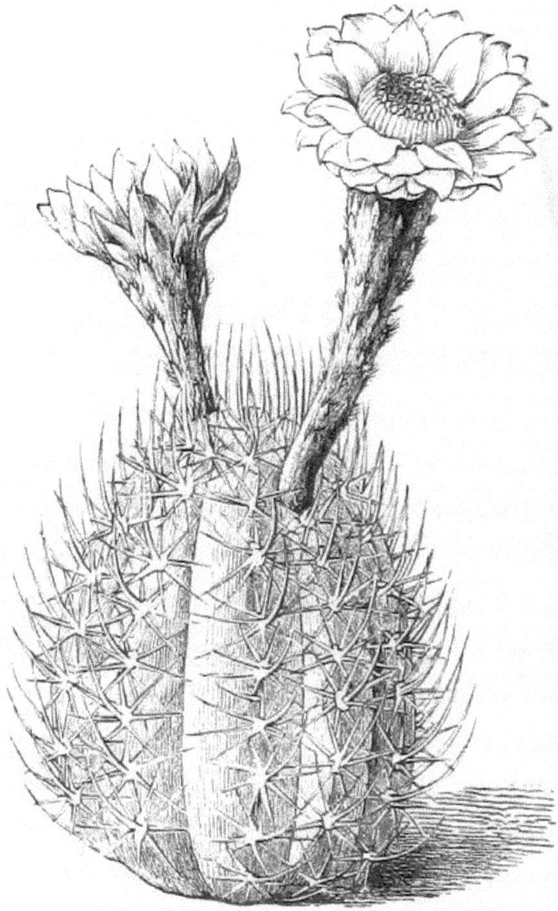

Fig. 11. Melonenkaktus.

LIMITATIONS

***

III

Everyone desires more than I give him. unrestricted happiness power reason to hope respect

What is left is far harder to bear.

15

Wandering hearts

***

We feel like strangers,
Roaming in the night,
Landing kisses on the wall,
Narrowly missing each other
Like we're playing
Pin The Tail On The Donkey.
We have terrible aim.

We stage a game of telephone,
Twirling the bright red
Pretend cord around our fingers,
Cutting circulation,
Filling in all the words
Lost along the way.
We easily find a disconnection.

We're terrible at this game.
Ad lib romance of insecurities,
You to me, Me to you,
Lost in the translations
Of absent-minded doodles
Spread across the pages of an old
Phonebook.
Was this where we went wrong?

We trace little love notes
Hidden between the ad listings of
Seeking Adventurer and Must Love Books.
Standards, values, beliefs, and emotions,
Shrunken to .5 font
Wedged in sight, out of mind.
Tiny little cracks within the pavement to
Break our backs - and our hearts.
We wander knowingly in the dark.

Lovers

***

There are two kinds of lovers in the world: the ones who stay, and those who leave. Growing up as a poor kid in the middle of nowhere, she'd been told to find the kind of man who'd stay. Forever and ever, the kind of man who would be hers.

Her mama said,
"you find a man who will make a good father, unlike your father."
Her siblings said,
"you find a man who makes good money and takes care of you."
Her friends said,
"you find a man willing to put up with you and your flaws."
Strangers said,
"you find a man of god" or "don't look for anyone except yourself."
Society said,
"just find someone, or you'll find no one at all."

No one thought to say, "Go out into the world. Find out the kind of woman you are. " No one said there was a third kind of love, a beautiful sort of emotions unfolding and twisting inside her like a swarm of butterflies, a pit of coiled serpents, a sheet of shadow half-draped over her naked heart: self-love.

XVI Carnations

Hornet's nest

***

Her body is a hornet nest; it hums with a warning, it clings to whatever its paper form can mold itself to. Unravel it - crack it open, and you'll witness every place where every thought burrowed deep, every worry sinking stingers where eyes can't easily see.

Becoming

***

You ever feel as if you are falling out of destiny? As if you are spiraling into a million directions, forced out from the center of who you are? The shards of my own identity imploded and exploded all at once, casting away any previous illuminations. It doesn't feel particularly good. But sometimes it feels right.

It is right in all the wrong ways.

I am not a vessel

***

I am not a vessel for you to fill; I am not a cog in your expectation machine.
I am not a woman who is owned by her husband or a female trapped by her biology; I am not an animal enslaved to my impulses.

I am not a person for you to define as "pretty" or "smart" or "impressionable" - a force quick to change her mind as time slips by. I am not playful when I say "NO" nor ignorant for choosing different; I am not a mirror of you, of men, of other women.
I am myself and I have my own desires.
I am not a vessel for you to fill, brim overflowing with old-fashioned expectations of children and family life. I am not a woman who is owned by her biology, who caves to someone who begs for me to "have a baby" just because it's the natural next step.

Because the natural next step for me is to have a career. It is to travel, to learn as many languages as I can, to write as many books as my soul wishes. It is to live the life my ancestors might have wanted, but could never have. I want to be
selfish
rebellious
knowledgeable
sensual
independent
vocal
empowered

Everything you think I shouldn't be.

NGARIAN FAIRY TALES
BY
Baroness Orczy
and Montagu Barstow.
SE charming Fairy Tales have
een very carefully selected
ollections of the
Magyar folk - lore
as told by the old
ian writers, many
se tales form the
vourites of the nurseries of
This volume undoubtedly
one of the best and most
lly got up Fairy Books ever
hed. Each page is illustrated
e or more artistic illustrations
ta- ented
of the
s Orczy and Mon-
rstow, reproduced in
OLD
OLD HUNGARIAN

Under siege

***

I do not want to know you. You are not someone I want to care for or be there for because I already feel like an overcrowded ship. I can barely set sail from the weight and I struggle, tirelessly, against the wind.

But you are ignorant. You simply do not know the effort it takes to carry you with me.
You and everyone else, who thanks me for having you in my life, are unbelievably blind to the struggle.

I want nothing more for my mast to break, for the wooden floors beneath your feet to cast you out at sea. Do I need you? Do I need all of you? Do I need *any* of you? All I can taste is the salt in the air. All I can feel are the splitters you drive into my skin each time you just don't get it.

You're too heavy, a burden, lead in my heart, and I want nothing more than for you to get the hell off my ship.

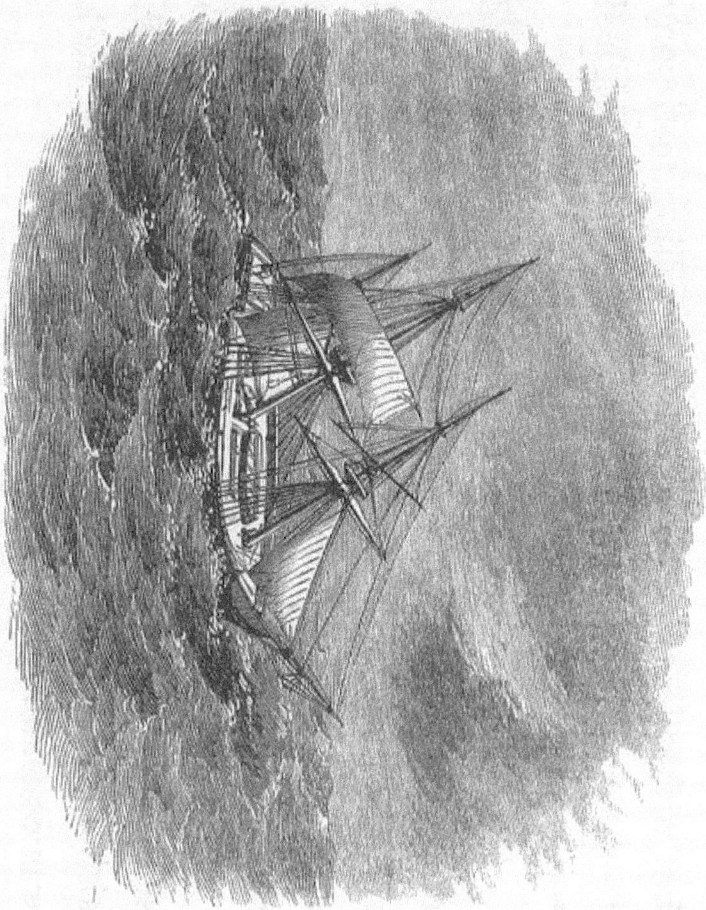

H.M.S. "Resolute" lying-to in the North Atlantic.

Hope

***

~~July 15, 1944: Its a wonder~~ I ~~havent~~
~~abandoned all my ideals, they seem~~
~~so absurd and impractical. Yet I~~
cling to ~~them because I still believe,~~
~~in spite of~~ everything, ~~that people~~
~~are truly~~ good ~~at heart.~~
~~Its~~ utterly impossible ~~for me to build~~
~~my life on a foundation of chaos,~~
~~suffering and death.~~ I see the world
~~being slowly transformed into~~ a
wilderness, ~~I hear the approaching~~
~~thunder~~ that, ~~one day,~~ will destroy
us ~~too, I feel the suffering of mil-~~
~~lions. And yet, when~~ I look ~~up at the~~
~~sky, I somehow feel that everything~~
~~will change~~ for ~~the better, that this~~
~~cruelty too shall end, that~~ peace ~~and~~
~~tranquility will return once more.~~

The Anatomy of Memory

***

Memories are cut into bones.

They are carved milestones adorning the doorway of my heart, holes chiseled into an instrument my fingers clutch.

With every breath, they sing. With every movement, they upset the dust that has settled, the sediment of emotion buried, I thought, at the back of my mind.

They haunt the passages of my lungs, and delight in my reaction:

a pause,
a sunken trance of reliving a singular
snapshot of an unfamiliar life entangled by red
string,

an irresistible urge to laugh through
the burning of eyes.

Graffitti

***

This mask is not brick & mortar graffitti.
I am,
Whoever you see.
Whoever they see.
Whoever I see.
Layers of paint,
grime,
wild ivy.

A collaborative interpretation

No one can agree on.

Fruhling des Bedauern

***

The Sun sets, I
Lay these bones to rest,
Beneath the words, etched,
"It's for the best."
I try hard to breathe, you
Oddly comfort me.
With liquor and lies, I
Can't bring myself to say,
It's okay, it's okay.
Night turns into day, I
Begin to turn away, You've
Become the grave,
Of everything I failed to say.

City soup

***

Foul- mannered words slid
Off my tongue, easily.
Greeted by a whirlwind of color -
A bright green bus breezing by,
Dirt and ash blown into my eyes,
And the inevitable splash of a puddle,

Which danced upon the curve,
Meeting me in a wet embrace.

Fences

***

I stood by the fence in my yard, little hands with splinters, and dreamt I was across the road, a normal child on a normal day. Hours were spent climbing an old sap, wrapping my legs around the branches, clinging to the story my own imagination had created.

I fell from the limb that day. I landed on my back, where I struggled for air as it left me and tears burned my eyes.

That was the day my mother returned and everything changed.A childhood, a blur of another time filled with seashells, gasoline, and tree climbing.

A collage of playing house with him, as he brushed my hair, stroked my cheeks, and touched me. Here, there. Places unseen but always felt. Unnoticed but always known. A melted pot of belts hitting flesh in the form of punishments, in words being used as knives, and the fence, in the yard, where I once played in my little dress, growing taller, bolder.

We left. My mother took us away to Florida, a place of sun and sand. A place, she said, for peace. A fresh start, a new beginning, a clean slate. In Florida, we had a new fence, which grew impossible to escape. The melting pot, the collection of endless experiences stirred round and round

As boyfriends abused, absent mothers ignored, medications were given to treat, the symptoms of the day, The symptoms, which in reality, were nothing more than a deterrence. A lie to hide the truth of child abuse and poor choices made by those too afraid to face them.

It was clear that the only way to obtain peace was to tell the truth. The only way to let go, was to open my angry fists and reveal what was already known but ignored: The bruises would speak for themselves. The emotions would illustrate all that had gone wrong in a little yellow house in the woods surrounded by a fence.

A fence too tall for a child to crawl over but I was not a child anymore. On the other side of the fence, there was a latch, one I couldn't see before that read,

> "There is peace when you understand, when you accept that it was not your fault."

Loaded heart

***

This is my heart,
It isn't whole.
It isn't open.
It's rigged with a
Self-destructive
Button.
No matter how much
You love me -
My finger is on the
Trigger.

Persistence

***

By night, I am
Water.
I glow
And run
And wish
To get in.

Needs

***

Love is like fire;
if it cannot find oxygen,
it will die.

You can't erase it

***

It never happened,

eventually

Eleutheromania

***

You're always leaving me. You make it hard
to stay, to breathe.

I hear the pounding of my heart,
a series of uncertain knocks in my chest.
Is anyone home?

No, we've camped out for the nighttime,
underneath a canopy of trees.

I wait for him to break the silence again. I sense his smile in the darkness, his soft laughter. Its gentleness i s at odds with his tight arms around me.

Our faces are tipped to the celestial night,
our fingers laced, our whispers becoming fog,
Gone by dawn.

›artie ombrée de la lune, près de la limite de l'om-
'e, se montrent fréquemment des points lumineux

ne
les
de
la
ıns
ır-
ıus
la
à
les
ta-
se,
r.,
les
›rs
›nt
ses
et
rès
m-
ıı-
'e -
ta-
en
es-

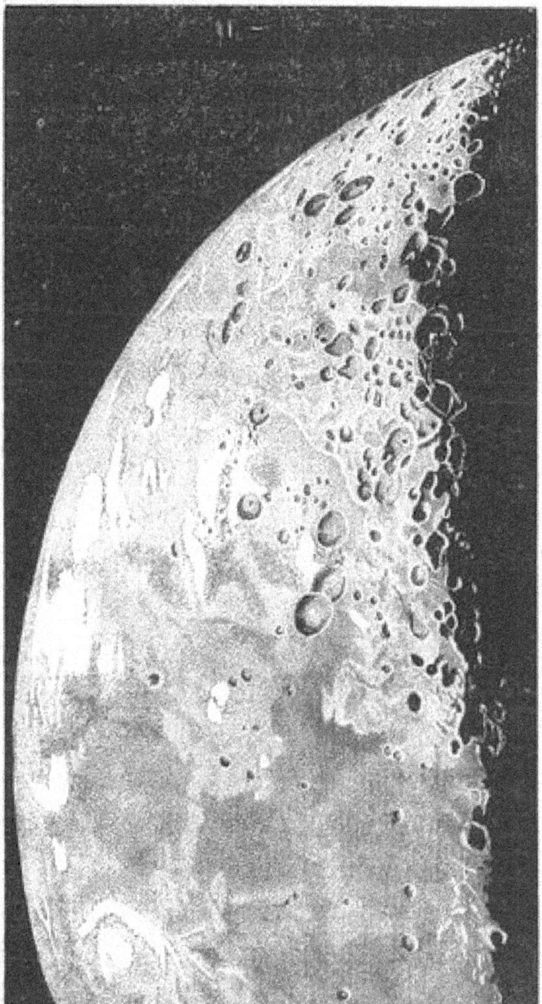

s et vingt-deux au-dessus de 4,800 mètres, hauteur
plus grande hauteur qu'ils aient déterminée est

Keep it to yourself

***

Keep it to yourself/ if you find my choice of/
love repulsive, don't say it aloud/ If you disagree
with my reproductive rights/ turn your eyes/
and check yourself.

If you can't get over the color of my skin/
my occupation/my beliefs/ where I live/
keep it to yourself/ if you know nothing
about me, what are you talking about?

Wear out my name and stuff words in my
mouth/ if you know nothing at all/
check yourself.

If you have nothing nice to say/
keep it to yourself/ if I live in a way
you dislike/ if I chose a path you don't
think is right/ if you prefer the day and
I, the night/ Are these differences worth
a fight?

You look for enemies in familiar faces/
Evil in the best of places/ terrorism in
vaginas, hijabs, visas, gender/ Your fear
defines the line where truths blur/ if
you're unsure/ if you have a doubt/
check your privilege/ check yourself

Don't spread your hate/
keep it to yourself.

Just say no

***

He kissed me with grass-flavored lips, eyes
bloodshot and swimming. An iris pierced
me and I wondered how I could love a

stoner, a weed-head, an introvert shrouded
in smoke and the flavor of mown lawns.

He discovered air and whispered
about luck and timing and the sound
of our hearts beating, erratic, unreasonable.

I couldn't keep up with the banter and his
wandering eyes that traveled the landscape
of my form.

I kissed him, shooing away Nancy
Reagan's "Just Say No" campaign and did
whatever felt right.

A jolt of electricity surged through me as his
tongue grazed my lip and I couldn't help but
wonder how the bitterness of grass could taste
Sweet.

Amaranthine

***

A brief visitation with old
Mute memories of winter in 1997.
Afflicted with a fever for freedom, a
Rantipole girl cloaked in the dark with
Apricity, chased anonymity into pines.
Naked intention afforded by the night.
The clandestine promise of wild green
Hills, gypsy caravan summers, and
Indigo sunsets finger painting the horizon.
Nobody would miss the rantipole girl who
Embraced the unknown to find herself.

Finder's fee

***

The headline reads:
"Loved one missing. Finder's fee."
And we wait, wait, wait.
For the end of the beginning,
Or was it the beginning of the end?

It might all be in my head.

A paperboy shouts in the street,
Suspicious of anyone he meets,
"Have you seen this person?"
I whisper back into the milk carton,
"Have you seen me?"

And we repeat, repeat, repeat.

White milk mustache dreams,
Dancing barefoot in the streets,
Singing loudly until we can't breathe,
And for a moment,
You see me, me, me.

Or so the headline reads.

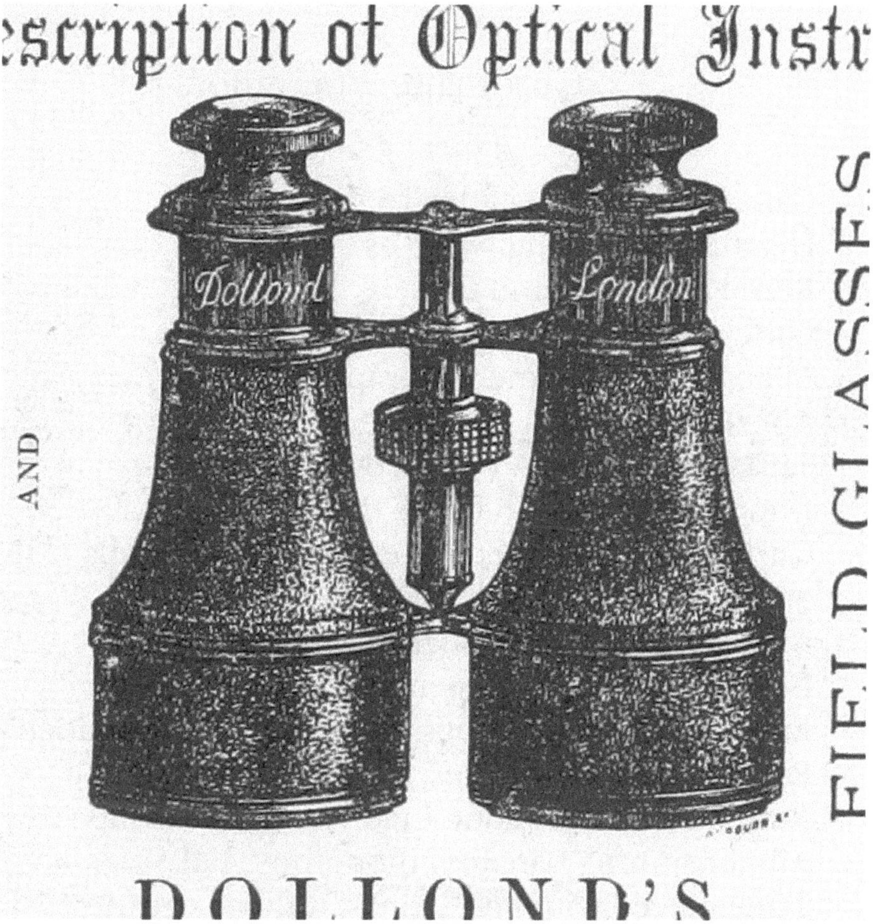
of Optical
Dollond
London
AND

Chromatic Aberration

***

Calling all escapists, I heard the
Headlines speaking to me as
Remy and Riley and that
Other chick whose name began with
M kept watching me with rapt
Apprehension.
Time of your lives, I echoed the TV
Impostor, the beach bottle babe
Curling her finger like an enchantress, a wink.

After throwing my things in a suitcase,
Before the fever for fleeing set in,
Excuses fall like wet rags, concerns like misguided
Rail trains, paper planes, filler fabled what ifs.
Run, I wanted to shout. Live your lives. Escape this
All-consuming banality, monotony, sad
Tune played with taut strings, unlived dreams.
Imagine yourself outside this white picket fence
Out in the world, over the moon, outrunning the slow
Nothings that take place in this old farm town.

Alleyway

***

I miss you. These words are
what I tell myself as I
Exit the room.

These walls are dull.
These halls are grey.
This heart is numb.
You were my life.

I wish I could miss you. These words
Are what I should say, should feel
Between my ribs like pounding fists
against the wall.

I leave or I'm left, my hands
Gripping the frame.
I'm afraid that if I let go,
The part of you inside me will die.

These walls will fall away,
These halls will disappear,
You will be gone.

This heart will be homeless
In an alley somewhere,
Bickering with a stray cat
About all the ways
I went wrong.

Logophile

***

I dream in the cover of books,
between the lines and half-dazed looks.
I dream in words I can't pronounce;
I use them all to build a house.

est of George street, he was partially de- | The subject of the engraving is the house
ented, or perhaps, as the modern term | Mr. William Knott, the grandfather of Ca

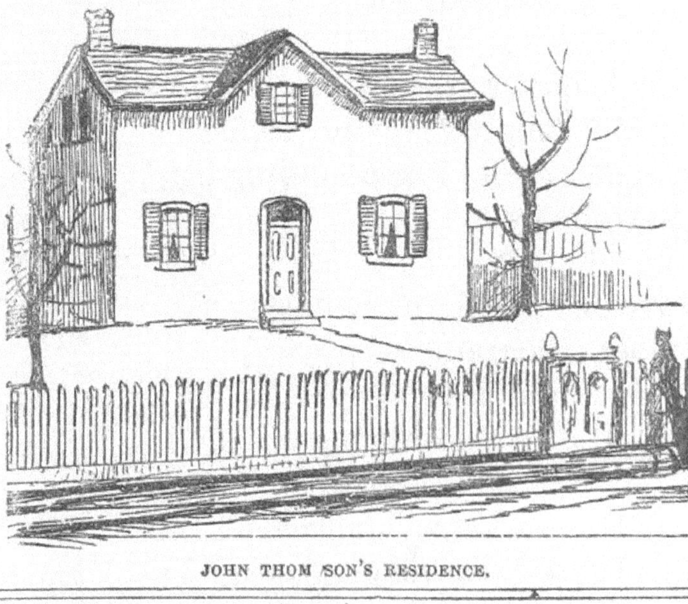

JOHN THOMSON'S RESIDENCE.

Depression

***

Sometimes I am afraid I'll never be rid of this feeling- the lack of desire, of motivation, of anything really. Though I have many ideas, they feel more like echoes and memories, rather than living, breathing parts of me. I'm afraid I'll start to disappear behind this emptiness.

Smile

***

I stare into the charcoal sky,
I feel you next to me and I,
Never thought to question why,
I smile each time I catch your eye.

Ruined

***

Come back to me, I

Simply couldn't see, Blind

The arrant symmetry, You

Were my everything.

You opened me, sigh

To the endless sea, I

Simply couldn't breathe,

When you looked at me.

We broke apart, You

And your paper heart, grew

Like frosted grass, Love

I ruined you.

The Perfectionist

***

You are all that that I see and nothing I want.
I am a harsh critic of everything you do.
I judge your existence and degrade you each time I find
flaw. I am a perfectionist and you,
You are terribly imperfect.
You remind me of barely legible handwriting,
Of chipped paint in the window sill.
When I look at you, I think of storms that ruin a beautiful
day. You're chaotic, helpless, ignorant, and oblivious.
You lack self control.
You are all that I see and nothing I want.
Yet, I'm conflicted and unable to take you apart; to unwire
you. Despite a deep discontent with you - regret and
unhappiness- I find I love you in unexpected ways.

I appreciate your resilience, the perseverance you possess.
I'm fond of your passion, though sometimes easily
misplaced and disastrous. You perceive this world in vivid
color and your compassion evokes a response in me,
A feeling of something forgotten but not quite lost.

You are beautiful, passionate, unyielding,emphatic.
You are terribly imperfect. I find myself in a cognitive
dissonance, both in loving and hating you.

I am unable to take you apart, reassemble you until you are
perfect; All the parts must be in harmony. Yet, when I look
into you, I see you're already the way you're meant to be.
The parts, though out of harmony, cannot be upgraded.
The system cannot be reprogrammed. In a sense, you are
perfect and this confuses me.
If you are perfect, then am I?

ORIGAMI

***

You remind me of
Paper dolls in the summer
Origami sin.

Los Angeles

***

Los Angeles and Tilda have a lot in common.
It's a land of loose angels and she's slack as can be.
An alleyway of lost abilities and limp acceptances.
Tilda takes it like a dog, labored "ahs" bouncing off
Red bricks caked in grime as she loses absolution.

Yes, Los Angeles and Tilda share a deep connection.
Lingering aspirations thick and sticky as humid air.
Tilda huffs and puffs but her lungs abandon inflation,
leaving acrid gasps of smoke, a vodka soaked tongue to
Light a fire in the wetness of her lapis eyes.

Los Angeles will strip her clothes from the bones of her
Shoulders, leveling absurd expectations to the sewage bed,
Where Tilda will beg like a nomadic lover abandoned.

Lazy accusations, lacquered ambitions, labial assimilation,
Languorous affections, lackluster alabaster face of Tilda,
Loose angel from Philadelphia who came to learn acting
in Los Angeles.

It's a land of lacy amateurs, laxative amoebas, leggy anatomies
With size 2 waist lines and botox-dotted barbie dolls sprawled
Over pristine steel slabs of metal where they list acrimonious
Reasons their bodies have failed them.

Tilda was one of them. She was a loose angel roaming the streets,
looking around for a sign of belonging, losing ambition like
A peacock squanders feathers.It's no wonder at all that
Los Angeles and Tilda have a lot in common.

L
A

If it's worth it

***

Forget about the scars she left
as white-hot reminders on your skin.

Forget the dreams you held with keen
anticipation on the tips of your fingers.

Forget the sensation of luke-warm rain falling,
head-over-heels to the Earth, where it nurtured
all your failed hopes.

Forget the sound of her breath as you
make love to her at 4:00 am.

Her arms,
a hesitant cage,
released you moments too soon.

Forget the nosy walls who listened to
arguments and emotions spent, in vain,
to reclaim a love that was never yours.

Forget about the scars she left
as spider veins in the foundation of
your soul, a disorienting map of truth
entangled with lies.

If at all possible,
forget, forget, forget.

V

***

V

we

demand to be believed

important

valued

deeply

enriched.

regarding

things in this world.

to have been there

on the shore

convinced of

cor-

rectness

Desire

***

The error is in the way I see you,
The shadows you cast against me,
As we lean into each other and whisper,
Secrets only an affair can taste.

Error in the lips that press against me,
In the hands that cling to old memories,
The skin that I can't distinguish from my own.

Eyes that undress me from across the room,
The smile that has conditioned me to know
To own the madness of false hope and yet,
Anticipate the fall that would send me,
Shattering into a million pieces upon the floor.

Hurricane

***

All we know is the hurricane/
falling, colliding, unforgiving rain/
churning and twisting and drowning/
consumed by the sirens of blame/
boarding up windows/
refusing to change.

21st street

***

She's sure he didn't mean to call her boring
He was probably joking, even.
Yet, as he turned away from her and announced it
Loudly to the small audience of their friends,
She felt a little piece of herself chip,
A small sensation she has come to recognize
As her feelings being hurt.

She sat there, hands clasped in her lap,
Waiting. And waiting.

She hopes he will say something to her
Take notice, care.

Yet, all she want is to leave; she wants to cry.
She wants to cry.

Anxious Soul

***

She called it a ghost; a phantom pain that ached, invisible, near nonexistent. Like an organ, visceral, wounded, a bleeder freely flowing; constant thoughts of what ifs and she needed to hear words outside her body to catch her breath; only when said aloud did "I'll be okay" make any sense.

Muse

***

Then, I decided I no longer wanted a muse. Because none could compare to the first. But no matter how far I searched for him again, the closest I ever came to him was my reflection in the mirror.

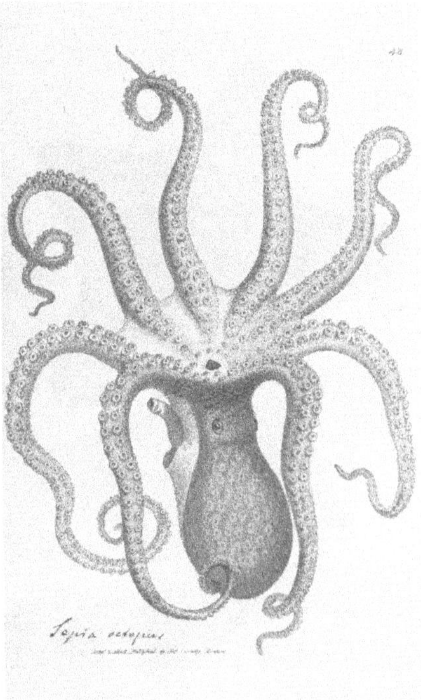

How we end

***

We are not forever. Your eyes open and I see myself in them, but I am alone in a sea of blue. Your hands against the bare of my skin, barely touch, as your map the way to broken hearts across my collar bone.

I close my eyes and tilt my heart back. I want to say where it hurts. We watched the sun set, pale lavender draped in tangerine and pastel pinks - a soft hush of the world as you inhaled, lips curled around a question you already had the answer to.

You asked how two people in love, wrapped in thin sheets, hearts pounding like the drums of war - how could people like us not be forever? How can love, which once filled us beyond measure, bleed out leaving us bleached and worn and silent.

Neither of us dared to answer. We laid there in the dying glow of light, fingers laced together, lips pressed in a prayer. Two hearts clinging to the only place they've known,
But no one's home.

All I know is this

***

I cannot tell you what my favorite color was
but I could list the shades of the pills I swallowed.
I can sing them like the alphabet, and
Chant all the side-effects that followed.

I cannot tell you where I ended up
but I could admit where I always wanted to be.
I can show you a picture of when I was ten,
though the dream never became a reality.

I cannot tell you where the time went
but I know it abandoned me in a blur.
I cannot say if childhood was bliss at all,
Was she me? Am I her?

I don't know if time heals all wounds
but I know the phantom ache of loss remains.
I could trace the fine white scars from here to there,
Wondering - if I spoke out, if I defied, if I learned to leave
Or dared to stay
- would anything have changed?

Reckless Abandon

***

Bare feet cut up by the glass.
Pale skin littered with beach sand.
An ocean wind drowning the sound
  of goodbye as it leaves my lips.

Mother wore a summer dress.
Knot bound at the base of her neck.
She smiles, teeth cracked and eyes closed.
  It's obvious she's losing her breath.

Sister and Father chase each other,
weaving around dunes and washed up seaweed.
As Father catches her, laughter pierces the air.
Her hair unravels in the wind, tears of bliss mixing
  with the bitter, salt air.

    She's the only one here.

Gulls cry and waves carve the rugged terrain,
Moss covered knives greet the blue sky.
Soothing waves disguise a heaviness.
My feet are bleeding, my legs are trembling,

  the word falls dead - a whisper.

Mother waves at a stranger down the shore.
Father twirls sister in a perfect, unbroken circle.
My footprints dig into the sand, uneven,
malformed, filling with water and blood.

Proof of life, I suppose.

I sign my name into the sand.
A shell eclipses the final three letters.
I smile at the incompleteness,
It doesn't reach my eyes and I wander,
over the hill and out of sight,
the sun heating my back.

My shadow casts false promises,
As I disappear.

Undone

***

These little acts undo,

Each weave that holds me still.

I pull air into my lungs,

Bite my lips against the chill.

The emptiness consumes,

Yet fills each crack within my bones.

I'm tearing at the seams,

Within the skin I called my home.

Things I should tell you

***

I've found bravery in the cold, crisp night and the truth is, I love you. Since the day I met you, my entire life has changed. It's not like before, when I loved someone as if they were the center of my universe. No, I love you enough to share the universe with you.

I love you and so I make room, in the chaotic untidiness, in the warm morning cuddles, and the space beside my toothbrush and I know there's a chance that this could end, I don't even think about it because you're here with me now and that is all that matters. It's hard enough to love myself and you help me to see all the reasons why I should appreciate what I have to offer the world.

You love me as I am and you encourage me to go out into the world, to learn and to conquer, and each time I feel you behind me, hands on my shoulders, a tender urging to just be myself, I fall in love more deeply.

Loose Connection

***

We are the sum of our interactions;
Debris lost in a vacuum of space.

PLANETS, THEIR ARCHITECTURE. 279

zone nearer the sun, the boundaries of which are not well

DOUBLE SPIRAL NEBULA.

defined. It is shaped somewhat like a quoit. The sun

Kintsugi

***

I am done asking the world to accept the parts of me it helped to break. There is nothing wrong with being a little shattered. From this angle, the pieces look like glitter in the lighting, and I like it.

ENCORE:

EXCERPTS FROM A SPARK IN THE NIGHT

Overcome

***

I cannot express the shards of my soul.
You held the fragments of me between your lips,
As I stood on the edge of my sanity, and I,
I drown inside the chambers of your chest,
I fight to breathe beneath the weight of your gaze,
I struggle to find my strength as I dissolve into you.
And I cannot recall, imagine, or fathom,
When I last existed singularly.

Shades of blue

***

At the table I sit and stare, I'm on the very edge of this wicked chair.

And it's such a lovely trap, this game we play. Each piece we give and give, is another that we take. I dry my eyes, darling, dry them soaking wet, and I shattered my lungs as I try to catch my breath and I'm swallowed whole by these shades of blue.

Swallowed, chewed, and spit out by the hungry mouth of you.

I love the way I hate you

***

I count the ways I love you. I count them till bleed. And even when the battle's over, it's not enough for me.

I spit the words and watch the burn, black holes into your heart. I wonder why you stand there, I wish we were apart.

I burn your clothes to kill scent, that wrote memories across my bed. I scream into the shower head. I scream words I never said.

Words that say a thousands things, ones that mean nothing now.I count the ways I love you. I count them till I drown.

I love the way I hate you. I hate the way I stay. I can't stand the way you won't go, even when it's all too late.

I count the ways I love you. I count them till I bleed. And even when the battle's over, it's still not enough for me.

Welcomed lies

***

Say it to me, Love.
Replace the distance,
With your skin and lips.
All your little tricks,
Make me forget,
That we're wearing,
Tearing at the seams.

The
End
BRITISH
5 MA 87
MUSEUM

ACKNOWLEDGEMENTS

Thank you to all of my closest friends and family. You have given me a home in your hearts & accepted my words without judgement. Without your amazing encouragement & support, I would not have had the courage to put pen to paper.

To the cover designer (& friend) Katharine Manolios, who breathed vivid life into *Elsewhere, We Became* with her beautiful art.

To Harry, who saw the best in me when I was at my worst & spoke up for me when I couldn't find my voice. You were the *best* caseworker any foster kid could hope to have. *RIP*.

Lastly, a massive thank you to all my wonderful readers, whose loyalty, courage, and uniqueness inspire me everyday.

ABOUT THE AUTHOR

Ari Augustine wears many hats. She is a writer, a poet, an editor, and, as of 2018, a co-founder of CraftQuest, a live Youtube webinar series for writers.

In 2014, she published a brief collection of poetry entitled *A Spark In The Night*, which received several stellar reviews and tackled the tough topic of mental health.

Her writing is best described as darkly lyrical and refreshingly blunt.

Ari currently resides in Seattle, Washington with her partner in crime, Chris, and their imaginary pet chameleon, Tagkoe.

ABOUT THE COVER-DESIGNER

Katharine Manolios is a Pittsburgh-based illustrator and graphic designer specializing in various mediums including watercolor, pen and ink, Adobe software, photography, and acrylic painting.

Katharine is employed at the Community College of Allegheny County as a visual graphic artist and is majoring in Graphic Communications. As a designer, she loves to incorporate a wide array of themes into her art and to work closely in collaborations with her clients.

To find out more about Katharine Manolios, please visit her Instagram: https://www.instagram.com/katherinemanolios/

ABOUT THE ILLUSTRATIONS

The images included in *Elsewhere, We Became* do not belong to the poet or the cover designer. All, but one image in this poetry collection were obtained through The British Library Flickr page, where the organization offers access to public domain illustrations that have no known copyright restrictions.

The poet urges you to explore the amazing historical artwork generously provided freely to the public by The British Library:

https://www.flickr.com/photos/britishlibrary/albums

Lightning Source UK Ltd.
Milton Keynes UK
UKHW02f0616040718
325208UK00006B/657/P

9 780692 097823